THE PERIODIC TABLE

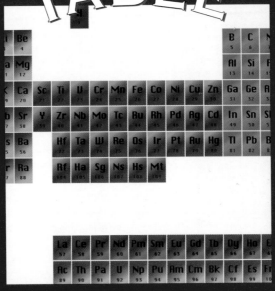

A TRUE BOOK®

by

Salvatore Tocci

Children's Press®
A Division of Scholastic Inc.

New York Toronto London Auckland Sydney
Mexico City New Delhi Hong Kong
Danbury, Connecticut

This bracelet is made of silver, which is one of the elements listed on the periodic table.

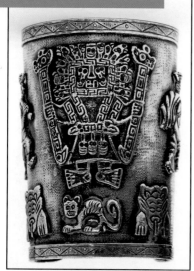

Reading Consultant
Julia McKenzie Munemo, EdM
New York, New York

Content Consultant
John A. Benner
Austin, Texas

The photo on the cover shows the Periodic Table. The photo on the title page shows part of the Periodic Table.

The author and the publisher are not responsible for injuries or accidents that occur during or from any experiments. Experiments should be conducted in the presence of or with the help of an adult. Any instructions of the experiments that require the use of sharp, hot, or other unsafe items should be conducted by or with the help of an adult.

Library of Congress Cataloging-in-Publication Data

Tocci, Salvatore.
The periodic table / by Salvatore Tocci.
    p. cm. — (A true book)
    Includes bibliographical references and index.
    Contents: Where do you sit?—How was the periodic table developed?—How is a periodic table organized?—How can a periodic table be divided?—Fun facts about the periodic table.
    ISBN 0-516-22833-1 (lib. bdg.)   0-516-27852-5 (pbk.)
    1. Periodic law—Tables—Juvenile literature. 2. Chemical elements —Juvenile literature. [1. Chemical elements.] I. Title. II. Series.
QD467.T63 2004
546.8—dc22
                                                                  2003016208

Contents

Students often have assigned seats because of a certain reason, such as their age or height.

Where Do You Sit?

Do the students in your classroom have assigned seats? If they do, your teacher probably had some logical reason for assigning students to their seats. For example, your teacher may have arranged the seats based on the spelling of students' last names. Perhaps your teacher arranged the seats based on students' height, with the shorter ones sitting in the front of the classroom. No matter what the method your teacher used when assigning seats, the students wound up sitting in some kind of logical order.

In the 1860s, a Russian scientist named Dmitri Mendeleev was trying to come up with a logical way to arrange the elements.

Russian scientist, Dmitri Mendeleev, the creator of the periodic table.

Everything in the universe is made of matter.

Elements are the building blocks of matter. **Matter** is the stuff or material that makes up everything in the universe. This book, the chair you are sitting on, and even your body, are made of matter.

Mendeleev was trying to arrange all sixty-three elements known at the time into a chart. He wrote the name of each element on a card, along with what scientists knew about the element. Mendeleev then studied the information on the cards, looking for some logical way to arrange the elements. He placed the cards into columns and rows and kept moving them around as if he were playing a game.

Finally, Mendeleev came up with an arrangement that made sense to him.

He noticed that in his arrangement, the elements in the same column had something in common with one another. For example, elements in the same column react, or behave, the same way when they are mixed with other elements. What Mendeleev had developed is known as the **periodic table** of the elements.

How Was the Periodic Table Developed?

In addition to a name, every element also has a symbol. The symbols for the sixty-three elements that Mendeleev organized are made of either one or two letters. A one-letter symbol is always written as an uppercase letter, such as

H for the element hydrogen. A two-letter symbol is always written with the first letter in uppercase and the second letter in lowercase, such as He for the element helium.

In addition to the symbols for every element, Mendeleev's table also had several blank spaces. Mendeleev included these spaces because he did not know of any element that he could fit into them. Instead, he predicted that elements

	I	II	III	IV	V	VI	VII		VIII	
I	H									
II	Li	Be	B	C	N	O	F			
III	Na	Mg	Al	Si	P	S	Cl			
IV	K	Ca	?	Ti	V	Cr	Mn	Fe	Co	Ni
V	Cu	Zn	?	?	As	Se	Br			
VI	Rb	Sr	Yt?	Zr	Nb	Mo	?	Ru	Rh	Pd
VII	Ag	Cd	In	Sn	Sb	Te	I			
VIII	Cs	Ba	Di?	Ce?						
IX										
X			Er?	La?	Ta	W		Pt	Ir	Os
XI	Au	Hg	Ti	Pb	Bi					
XII				Th		U				

This is how Mendeleev arranged the symbols of the sixty-three elements known at the time into a periodic table. Can you find the blank spaces he left? Hint: Look for the question marks.

would be found later that would fit perfectly into the spaces he had left. Scientists later discovered these elements. The discovery of these elements convinced many scientists to accept Mendeleev's periodic table.

Mendeleev organized his periodic table based on the information he had written down on the card for each element. This information had to do with atoms. An **atom** is the smallest unit of an element. An atom is so small that it can be seen only with the help of the most powerful micro-scopes. To appreciate how small an atom is, imagine that a golf ball is as big as Earth. Each atom that makes up this huge golf ball would only be the size of a normal golf ball.

Even though it is so small, an atom still has **mass**. Mass is how much matter an object has. For example, your mass is

This father, who weighs 160 pounds, has twice the mass of his daughter, who weighs 80 pounds.

all the matter or material that makes up your body. We usually compare masses in terms of weights. For example, a person who weighs 160 pounds (60 kilograms) has twice the mass of a person who weighs 80 pounds (30 kg). Because an atom is extremely small, it has an extremely small mass known as its atomic mass.

Mendeleev had written down the atomic mass of each element. He arranged the elements, starting with the one that had the smallest atomic mass. He then arranged the remaining elements in order

	I	II	III	IV	V	VI	VII	VIII		
I	H 1									
II	Li 7	Be 9.4	B 11	C 12	N 14	O 16	F 19			
III	Na 23	Mg 24	Al 27.4	Si 28	P 31	S 32	Cl 35.5			
IV	K 39	Ca 40	? 45	Ti 50	V 51	Cr 52	Mn 55	Fe 56	Co 59	Ni 59
V	Cu 63.4	Zn 65.2	? 65	? 70	As 75	Se 79.4	Br 80			
VI	Rb 85.4	Sr 87.6	Yt? 88	Zr 90	Nb 94	Mo 96	? 100	Ru 104.4	Rh 104.4	Pd 106.6
VII	Ag 108	Cd 112	In 113	Sn 118	Sb 122	Te 128?	I 127			
VIII	Cs 133	Ba 137	Di? 138	Ce? 140						
IX										
X			Er? 178	La? 180	Ta 182	W 186		Pt 197.4	Ir 198	Os 199
XI	Au 197?	Hg 200	Ti 204	Pb 207	Bi 210					
XII				Th 231		U 240				

The numbers represent the atomic masses of the elements.

of increasing atomic mass. This would be like a teacher who arranges students' seats based on their masses. The student with the smallest mass would be placed in the first seat, the next smallest in the next seat, and so on. Once a row was filled, students would be assigned seats in the next row until everyone had a seat.

Making a Periodic Table

Give each classmate an index card. Ask them to write down the following information on the card: date of birth, hair color, favorite food, favorite television show, amount of time spent each night doing homework, and number of siblings in their immediate family. Collect the cards and then arrange them so that the cards in each row or column have something in common.

For the most part, Mendeleev's periodic table made sense. Elements that had something in common were in the same column. However, Mendeleev sometimes had to bend the rules to make sure that all sixty-three elements were grouped correctly. For example, take a close look at his periodic table. Notice that Mendeleev placed Te before I. This was the only way to arrange the elements so that Te was in the same group with similar elements. However, Te should come after I because I has a smaller atomic mass.

The few problems Mendeleev had with his arrangement were solved by an English scientist named Henry Moseley. Moseley arranged the elements according to their atomic numbers instead of their atomic masses. An **atomic number** of an element refers to a specific part that makes up an atom's mass. A person's mass is made of many parts, such as the legs, arms, and head. An atom's mass is also made of many parts. One of these parts is called a **proton**. The number of protons determines an element's atomic number.

For example, an atom of hydrogen has only one proton. The atomic number of hydrogen (H) is 1. An atom of helium (He) has two protons. The atomic number of helium is 2. When Moseley arranged the elements by atomic number, everything fell into place. For example, Te, with atomic number 52, belongs before I, with atomic number 53.

How Is the Periodic Table Organized?

The name "periodic table" points out how the elements are organized. The word "table" shows that the elements have been placed into columns and rows. The word "periodic" indicates that the elements are arranged in a repeating pattern.

To understand what "periodic" means, assume that you have a collection of baseball cards of out-fielders from three teams. Now imagine that you take the cards from one team and arrange them in a row, starting with the left fielder, then the center fielder, and finally the right fielder. Next, you place the cards

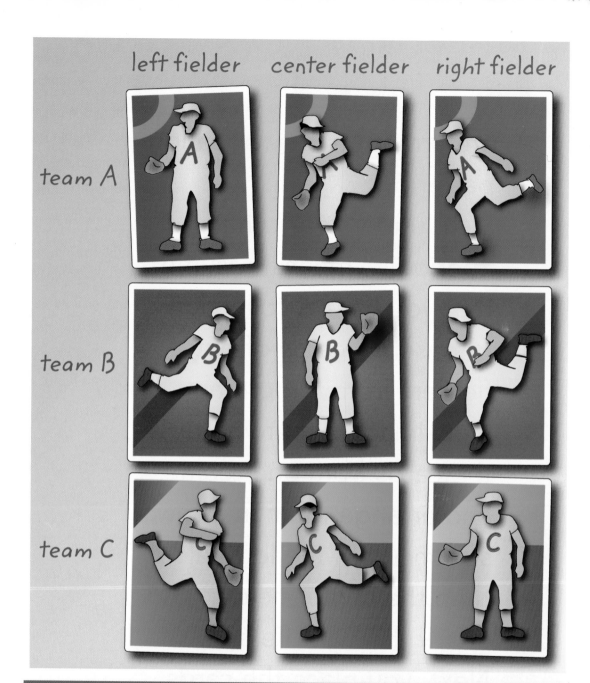

left fielder   center fielder   right fielder

team A

team B

team C

Notice that the baseball players in each row and in each column have something in common with one another.

from another team in the same order but in a new row under the cards from the first team. Finally, you do the same with the last team.

This periodic table of cards forms a repeating pattern. As you move from left to right starting at the top, you will go from a left fielder to a center fielder and then to a right fielder. This pattern will repeat as you move through the table. In this periodic table of cards, the columns show the players' position, and the rows show the players' team.

In a periodic table of elements, the columns are called **groups**, and the rows are called **periods**. Elements in the same group behave in a similar manner. For example, the elements sodium (Na) and potassium (K) are in the same group. Both these

Periodic Table of the Elements

	Group 1	Group 2	Group 3	Group 4	Group 5	Group 6	Group 7	Group 8	Group 9	Group 10	Group 11	Group 12	Group 13	Group 14	Group 15	Group 16	Group 17	Group 18
Period 1	1 H																	2 He
Period 2	3 Li	4 Be											5 B	6 C	7 N	8 O	9 F	10 Ne
Period 3	11 Na	12 Mg											13 Al	14 Si	15 P	16 S	17 Cl	18 Ar
Period 4	19 K	20 Ca	21 Sc	22 Ti	23 V	24 Cr	25 Mn	26 Fe	27 Co	28 Ni	29 Cu	30 Zn	31 Ga	32 Ge	33 As	34 Se	35 Br	36 Kr
Period 5	37 Rb	38 Sr	39 Y	40 Zr	41 Nb	42 Mo	43 Tc	44 Ru	45 Rh	46 Pd	47 Ag	48 Cd	49 In	50 Sn	51 Sb	52 Te	53 I	54 Xe
Period 6	55 Cs	56 Ba	57 La	72 Hf	73 Ta	74 W	75 Re	76 Os	77 Ir	78 Pt	79 Au	80 Hg	81 Tl	82 Pb	83 Bi	84 Po	85 At	86 Rn
Period 7	87 Fr	88 Ra	89 Ac	104 Rf	105 Db	106 Sg	107 Bh	108 Hs	109 Mt	110 Uun	111 Uuu	112 Uub		114 Uuq				

58 Ce	59 Pr	60 Nd	61 Pm	62 Sm	63 Eu	64 Gd	65 Tb	66 Dy	67 Ho	68 Er	69 Tm	70 Yb	71 Lu
90 Th	91 Pa	92 U	93 Np	94 Pu	95 Am	96 Cm	97 Bk	98 Cf	99 Es	100 Em	101 Md	102 No	103 Lr

More elements have been discovered since Mendeleev's time. A modern periodic table contains 113 elements organized into eighteen groups and seven periods.

elements produce an explosion when they are dropped in water. Elements in the same period, or row, have atoms that have a similar structure.

Two periods are much longer than the others. To keep the periodic table from becoming too wide, some of the elements in these two periods are placed below the rest of the table.

Comparing Elements

Fill two small glasses halfway with white vinegar. Tease apart some steel wool that does not contain any soap. Place the steel wool in one glass. Place a sterling silver utensil in the other glass. Allow the glasses to sit for at least one hour. Pour off the vinegar. How do the steel wool and the utensil look the next day? Sterling silver is actually a mixture of silver and copper. Silver and copper behave in the same way because these elements belong to the same group. Nothing happens when you place them in vinegar and then expose them to the air. Steel wool is made of iron, which is an element that belongs to a different group. Iron behaves differently and forms rust when it is mixed with vinegar and then exposed to the air.

How Can the Periodic Table Be Divided?

The periodic table can be divided in ways other than into groups and periods. For example, the elements can be divided into metals and nonmetals. All **metals** conduct electricity. Most of the elements are metals.

Pure gold is too soft to use for making jewelry. It is usually mixed with other elements to make it harder and stronger.

These elements include iron (Fe), copper (Cu), aluminum (Al), silver (Ag), tin (Sn), and gold (Au). Some metals, such as iron, copper, and aluminum, are used to make products people use every day, such as pots, electrical wiring, and foil wrapping. Other metals, such as silver and gold, are used to make luxury items, such as jewelry.

Nonmetals do not conduct electricity. The two nonmetals that are probably most familiar to people are oxygen (O) and helium (He). Most living things depend on the oxygen in the

A blimp can contain enough helium to fill more than ninety thousand party balloons.

air to survive. Helium is lighter than air and is used to fill balloons and blimps.

There are, however, six elements that are neither metals nor nonmetals. These elements are like metals in some ways and like non-metals in other ways. These six elements are called semiconductors because they conduct electricity better than nonmetals, but not as well as metals. Silicon (Si), the best-known semi-conductor, is used to make computer chips.

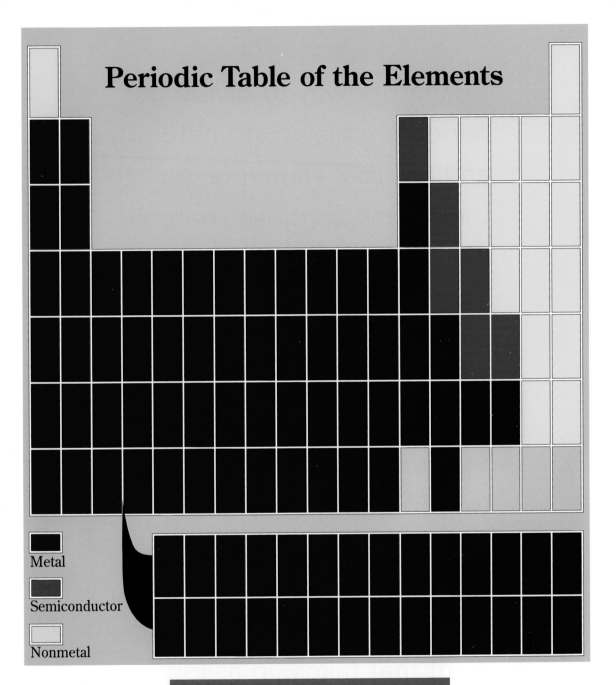

Periodic Table of the Elements

Metal

Semiconductor

Nonmetal

As these colors show, most elements are metals.

Another way to divide the periodic table is into natural and artificial elements. As their name suggests, natural elements are found in nature. There are ninety-two natural elements. Artificial elements are created in laboratories and are never found in nature. So far, scientists have created twenty-one artificial elements. Creating an element takes an enormous amount of energy. Today, scientists need equipment that takes up as much

space as a village to produce the energy needed to create an element. Artificial elements have a number of uses. For example, americium (Am) is used in home smoke detectors.

Fun Facts About the Periodic Table

- Tungsten (W) has the highest melting point (6192 degrees Fahrenheit or 3422 degrees Celsius) of any element. Tungsten is used to make the filaments in lightbulbs.

- The only letter that does not appear on the periodic table is J.

- Mercury (Hg) and bromine (Br) are the only two elements that are liquids at room temperature. Most elements are solids, while the rest are gases.

- The symbols for some elements are based on words from languages other than English. The symbol for gold, Au, comes from the Latin word for gold, aurum.

- The names for some elements honor famous scientists. For example, Einsteinium (Es) is named for Albert Einstein.

- The names for some elements are based on the location in which they were created. For example, berkelium (Bk) was named after Berkeley, California.

- The element sodium (Na) produces an explosion when added to water. The element chlorine (Cl) is a poisonous gas. However, if you put these two elements together, you get ordinary table salt, which is neither explosive nor poisonous.

To Find Out More

If you would like to learn more about the periodic table of elements, check out these books and web sites.

 **Books**

Bear, Jenkins and Magdalen Bear. **Chemical Helix: Make a 3-Dimensional Model of the Periodic Table.** Tarquin Publications, 1995.

Richardson, Hazel. **How To Split the Atom.** Scholastic, 2001.

Organizations and Online Sites

Elements
*www.chem4kids.com/files/
elem_intro.html*

Learn more about the elements by clicking on any one of eighteen shown on this site's periodic table. These eighteen elements were chosen because they make up most of the matter in the universe.

Word Search Puzzle
*www.stemilt.com/Kids/
PeriodicTablePuzzle.html*

Find the names of all the elements listed on the periodic table that are hidden in this puzzle, which has three levels of difficulty.

Pyrotechnics:
It's Elemental
*www.pbs.org.wgbh/nova/
kabooom/elemental/*

Highlighted in the periodic table shown on this site are the elements that are used in making fireworks. Click on these elements to see how they help make the colorful displays seen when fireworks explode.

Important Words

atom building block of elements

atomic number number of protons an
element has

element building block of matter

group vertical column of elements on the
periodic table

mass amount of matter an object has

matter material that makes up everything
in the universe

metal element that conducts electricity

nonmetal element that does not conduct
electricity

period horizontal row of elements on the
periodic table

periodic table organized arrangement of
all the elements

proton one of the particles that makes up
an atom

Index

Meet the Author

Salvatore Tocci is a science writer who lives in East Hampton, New York, with his wife Patti. He was a high school biology and chemistry teacher for almost thirty years. His books include a high school chemistry textbook and an elementary school series that encourages students to perform experiments to help them learn about science. As a chemistry teacher, he always emphasized to his students how much information can be found on the periodic table.